SUN PALACE

Ye Guangqin was born in Beijing in 1948, the thirteenth child of Manchu parents. During the Cultural Revolution she relocated to Shaanxi Province, where she worked as a nurse, and has been resident in Xi'an City for most of her life. Madame Ye's award-winning novel *Greenwood Riverside* was published in English translation by Prunus Press in 2011, and her collection *Mountain Stories* became the inaugural publication in Valley Press's Shaanxi Stories series in 2017.

This book is part of Shaanxi Stories, a series of translated works by acclaimed authors from the Shaanxi province of China, produced by Valley Press in collaboration with Northwest University, Xi'an. The series editors are Hu Zongfeng and Robin Gilbank. Other books in the series:

MOUNTAIN STORIES, Ye Guangqin
HOW OLD DAN BECAME A TREE, Yang Zhengguang
THE EARTHEN GATE, Jia Pingwa
THE BLOOD RED SUN, Wu Keijing
THE HOWL OF THE WOLF, Hong Ke
THE WILD LAND, Jia Pingwa
IRRATIONAL THINGS, Mu Tao
THE HOUR OF THE LOCUST, Yang Zhengguang

Sun Palace

YE GUANGQIN

*translated by Hu Zongfeng
and Robin Gilbank*

Valley Press

First published in 2022 by Valley Press
Woodend, The Crescent, Scarborough, YO11 2PW
www.valleypressuk.com

ISBN 978-1-912436-73-6
Cat. no. VP0194

A CIP record for this book is available from the British Library.

Text and cover design by Peter Barnfather.
Cover art: *Study of a Dog* (1860s) by Rosa Bonheur.
Series edited by Hu Zongfeng and Robin Gilbank.

Printed and bound in Great Britain
by Clays Ltd, Elcograf S.p.A.

Contents

Chapter One:
The Monk, the Cloth Doll, and the "Bonny Little Lass"

Before broaching the subject of Sun Palace, I should first share a few snippets about my family. We lived on Theatre Stage Lane, located to the east of the Lama Temple opposite the Imperial Academy and Chengxian Street. The alley ran from east to west, and was sedate and broad. All of the neighbours were familiar with each other and kept on good terms. Grandpa Zhao sold candles at the western entrance of the lane. The monk Guangyu from the Bolin Temple dwelt in the middle. Uncle Liu who kneaded cakes was to be found at the eastern entrance, with the stumpy tailor Sun Shun'er trading across from us. I counted every one of them among my fondest friends. All of them liked me and called me the "bonny little lass". They always talked about me as though I was the youngest girl in the alley even though that status came to be taken by another – namely Sun Shun'er's own daughter. She genuinely was the "bonny little lass".

This story begins when the baby in question was no more than one week old. She came into the world before she was ready and hadn't a clue how to suckle at her mother's breast. She only knew how to close her eyes and slumber. When his wife wasn't around, Sun Shun'er confided in me that they were uncertain whether their bonny little lass could survive. Her chances were slim and he feared for her mortality. I asked him what "mortality" was and he answered "death". I noticed that when Mr Sun spoke about the mortality of his bonny little lass there was not a hint of sadness about him. It was as if it was predestined.

I always went across the way to visit the bonny little lass. She was indeed tiny as a kitten. With her eyes squeezed shut and her head covered in small white blotches, her chicken feet-like hands clawed the air and her appearance was less than charming. My mother forbade me from visiting her. She would tell me that her mother was still in her confinement and that my swooping to and fro would be a nuisance. However, I couldn't restrain myself. I insisted that I just wanted to hold her in my arms for a while. There was no other motive and she shouldn't try and stop me.

Later, my mother sewed me a little doll of my own to nurse. The cloth dolly wore a flowery bonnet, had eyes that gazed like a dead fish and fake little red lips. I knew exactly how much cotton stuffing had been used to pad out her head and how much sawdust had been thumbed inside her body. Beneath her appealing exterior, she was a hotch-potch. Old Seven had painted her facial features with a brush. She was even uglier than the Sun family's bonny little lass. Old Seven was a dab hand at painting flowers and birds, but hopeless at doing faces. Thus, the doll had one big eye and one small and one eyebrow arched high while the other sank low.

Old Seven was the seventh of my elder brothers. He had no official job and drawing was his sole skill. He always stayed at home and never ventured out. By nature he was taciturn and introverted. No girl ever took a shine to him and he remained a bachelor even though he had come of age. This was a sore point where my mother was concerned.

One day, when I had virtually forgotten about the bonny little lass opposite, I heard sobs coming from her house. I wanted to go over and take a look, but was held back by my mother. When it was nearly lunchtime, I spotted Sun Shun'er stalking to the east with a freshly-carpentered, undecorated white box under his arm. From the grim expression on the tailor's face I could tell that his daughter had found her mortality. That wooden container was the casket for the bonny little lass. I verified all these matters by speaking with Old Zhang, our doorkeeper.

Old Zhang explained: "That type of coffin is known as a fire box. They are only used for children who have gone full-term and are destined for an unmarked grave. Otherwise people can burn them on a homemade pyre. They are not allowed to be buried in an ancestral plot." I asked him why that was. Old Zhang replied that it was because she was a "spirit not meant for this world". She had been born with the purpose of bringing trouble upon Sun Shun'er and perhaps she was a "bailiff" sent to settle a debt from a past life.

I asked my mama if I was a bailiff to which she replied that I was something of the sort. Then I retorted: "If that's so, I don't have to die. If you give me your loose change from time to time then we won't owe each other anything."

"Dream on."

The days passed by with an even patter. I found myself rendered tongue-tied, simply because there was nothing to occupy me. The courtyard marked the boundary of my world. I even had to beg my mother's permission to go out into the alley. She told me there were kid-snatchers who targeted tots. Their hands were daubed with a magic con-coction so that when they tapped victims on the head they became witless and followed them. The children would then be spirited away to be sold in the countryside, never to see their homes again. In modern parlance, these would be called child traffickers. They were in the business of bamboozling youngsters into being abducted. Sixty years ago, this was one of the eeriest things we feared. My activities within the courtyard were therefore limited. I had no pal to skip a rope with, no partner to throw and catch a beanbag with; all I could do was trill away to my cat. I sang 'Susan has Left Hongdong County', 'How Pretty is the Lassie on the Trike', and whatever else I was able to remember. I racked my brains and drew in my stomach until, to use a military phrase from back then, *I ran out of ammunition and provisions*. My repertoire was exhausted. The piebald kitten had no way of appreciating this. She would simply doze away on the step, snoring mellifluously.

Although the alley was extremely long, I had no playmate.

Sometimes, with Old Zhang the doorkeeper as my chaperone, I would go to the Bolin Temple. The Bolin Temple was a spacious complex built in the Yuan Dynasty. It was formerly one of the Eight Premier Temples in Beijing and a saying went, "First came Bolin, then followed Peking". It had the epithet "ten-mile Bolin" on account of its size. Despite its gradual shrinkage, the name remained.

According to my memory, the Bolin Temple was very roomy and contained several grand halls with steep stairways and brick screens bearing refined friezes. The elm trees defied age. The magnificent characters on the board proclaiming "Eternal Bolin" must have been written by one of the emperors. The Bolin Temple left me with two impressions. One was that of grandeur; the other was that it was a ramshackle place. The interior was gloomy and there were innumerable cypress trees like cheerless old fogeys. It was devoid of joy. No abbot was in residence, only a handful of brethren. These were stragglers with the air of leaderless troops. Usually, each one was wrapped up in his own affairs. When religious rites were to be performed, they would assemble and share equally any boon that came their way.

Small as I was, I could tell that Guangyu was the head of the order. Guangyu's full name was Saka Guangyu. I suppose that his surname was originally Shi, since monks would choose a consecrated title beginning with the same consonant or syllable as their birth name. Old Zhang pointed out that all those who are admitted by the temple share the name Saka to show they are kindred of the original Buddha Sakayamuni. Sharing that surname signifies their absorption into the realm of Zen. Guangyu's secular surname was in fact Zhang. Old Zhang claimed that they belonged to the same clan. To be accurate, the monk was a nephew five times removed. They could trace their lineage back to the Zhang Family Village in Tangshan. I asked him what "five times removed" meant. The doorkeeper described how they had a common ancestor five generations ago. He and Guangyu shared a distant grandpa.

Guangyu was fond of small children; I could sense this from his eyes. All kids seem to have the capacity to tell with one glance whether a person likes them or not. In the grand Bolin Temple, Old Zhang and Guangyu would chatter freely in the Tangshan dialect. When Guangyu became excited he would even jump onto the bench, squat down and hitch up his vestment in a way that didn't befit a master. There was a kind of syrupy candle smell within his room. He offered me some sweetmeats and they had the same aroma. Maybe they had been touched by the Buddha?

The more I stayed in Guangyu's chamber, the more my interest dwindled. I came out and strolled around. In front of the Grand Hall stood the vertical tablet borne on the back of a stone turtle. I would ride on the turtle's neck and try to drive it to charge like a camel. Of course, the statue was incapable of running. My father told me that the stone-carrier was not actually a turtle. It was a creature called Bixi – one of the sons of the Chinese dragon. He was the seventh son of the dragon, born to shoulder burdens. That is why he was made to support the stone tablet. I asked my father how many sons the Chinese dragon had and he told me nine. The Chinese dragon sired nine males in total and none of them was alike.

"The dragon has two more sons than you do," I observed.

My father had seven sons; a feat which he complained made his head ache. Each of the seven boys was a good-for-nothing troublemaker.

I asked my father why the nine sons of the Chinese dragon shared nothing in common. He replied: "They are just the same as your brothers. Every one has a different nature and a contrasting character and they cannot all sit together around a table. The eldest son of the Chinese dragon was named Qiuniu and he was fond of music. For this reason he is always carved on the heads of stringed instruments. The second son was named Yazi and he liked killing, so his image appears on the blades of swords and daggers. The third son was named Bi'an. Since he enjoyed lawsuits his likeness can be found crouching by the gates of a prison. The fourth son was named Suanni. As he liked swallowing smoke, you can find him carved into the eaves of a house. The fifth son, Taotie, was lazy yet relished good food ..."

"That one sounds just like me."

The nine sons of the Chinese dragon made me think of my own brothers. My father had seven sons. Among them were officials, teachers, clerks and even beggars. Each of them had their own home and their own child and their own life. Their lives may have run smoothly or been tough. Whether they were smooth or tough, they had one common trait, namely that none of them ever showed any concern towards me, their younger sister. Just like my father, they were always very busy, so busy that they never looked me straight in the face.

I was even lonelier than the turtle that carried the stone tablet.

Every year when summer came around, Beijing experienced storms. The heavy rains barraged down like somebody emptying a basin. I sat at the window watching the deluge. Colourful clouds chased like strands of smoke along the roofs of the eastern and western wing chambers. They seemed to be flying so low that they had actually landed on the rooftops. The one thing I most longed to do was to sit on the higher white banks of fluff. They would be as soft as heaped cotton. I could roll on them and somersault. Peering down from that lofty eminence, I was able observe my father going out to work and my mother stitching away. What else ought I to see? Nothing. Nothing more was to be added to those days of mine. That day the downpour was torrential. Water streamed down from the eaves, composing a curtain of rain. The courtyard was engulfed like a pavilion in a park.

Just as I became bored senseless, I caught sight of the straw-hatted Old Zhang wading through the mire in the yard. Overcome with excitement, I shouted at him from behind the glass: "It's raining, it's bubbling. Here comes the turtle in the straw hat!" The sound of the cascade was too emphatic for him to hear me. I called for him again and again and again until the veins in my neck were swollen.

My mama came out and stood beneath the porch. She handed a poker to Old Zhang. It turned out that there was a blockage in the drainpipe. Old Zhang jabbed away so that the courtyard might be emptied quickly. With his buttocks raised high, he gouged out refuse consisting of rotten branches and tree leaves. Most importantly, and most startlingly of all, was that my little cloth doll was among the recovered matter. Old Zhang picked up that ungainly toy and swung it angrily with a puttering sound. The poor little doll lurched onto the roof of the northern wing. She crawled along so that she could occupy a commanding position, where she could spy my father going out to work and my mother doing her stitching. The rainwater soon drained away. Old Zhang vanished. That little cloth doll disappeared. The courtyard was restored to its normal state.

Watching the rain, I grew more and more tired and could not keep my eyes open. Pat! My head bumped against the pane.

I overheard my mama nattering with Old Seven. She said we were going to lodge in Sun Palace for two days.

I was so glad at the prospect of going to Sun Palace that my heart nearly gave way with excitement.

Immediately, I felt cheerful.

Chapter Two:
The Earth Road, the Wasteland, and the Rickshaw

Sun Palace was not a famous place in Beijing, either in the past or in the present day. In my childhood, I talked to others about Sun Palace with pride, though nobody had heard of it. Nowadays, when I speak with someone about it, they will burble: "Well, it's a stop on the Tenth Circle Line of the Metro." They can say nothing more on the subject. Sun Palace – that once alluring, cordial and mysterious place – is unknown to the public. It has become part of my private trove. Whenever I think about it, I feel sorrow. I wrote this story in memory of Sun Palace. This is my mission in this world; I shall reveal my gratitude to it, together with the childhood expectations I had about this place.

Back then, Sun Palace was in the backwoods. My mother would spend days preparing for our visit. For Mama and me, the logistics of going there proved extremely important. You couldn't just spring to your feet and decide to undertake that journey. In my tedious life in the court-yard, the visit was a kind of open promise, a source of heartfelt joy, and a splendid festival. Such a chance only came around once a year.

In the 1940s, it took about half a day to travel there by rickshaw, going out of the Eastern Gate. It was not like today when people can reach the spot within a matter of minutes on the public bus. Every time we went, my mother would calculate the itinerary with great accuracy. We would spend two days on the visit, not a minute more nor a minute less. Those days would be free of wind and rain. At that time, there were no weather forecasts, so I do not know how she came up with her predictions.

Mostly, we went there in late summer or early autumn. The weather would be growing cool in the morning and the evening. All manner of fresh fruit sprang up on the markets. The temperature was neither sweltering nor nippy. It was a season when you could have your fill of playing and eating.

I loved this season.

Sun Palace was also my first point of contact with the land. From here, I came to know what the countryside was. I learned what compost is, what irrigation is, what weeding is, and what pinching-out is. Thus, when I grew up and was sent to live and work in the countryside as a member of a production brigade, I looked at the rivers and gullies, canals, yellow dogs and poplar trees without any sense of novelty.

On the day of our departure, Old Zhang hailed a rickshaw which halted in front of the gate. My mother would bargain with the coolie for some time because he was unwilling to drive to Sun Palace. Old Zhang had only told him that we were going out of the Eastern Gate without divulging our precise destination. When the coolie knew we wanted to go to Sun Palace, he made plain his reluctance and whinged that it was too out-of-the-way. The return journey without a passenger would wipe away his profit. My mother carried on mouthing niceties and promised to give him ten baked cakes. The coolie then caved in against his wishes.

In fact, Sun Palace could be reached by riding a donkey. There was a market immediately outside of the Eastern Gate where many donkeys were up for hire. Once an agreement had been cut, the owner of the beast would position a saddle-mat on its back and lead from the front. The customer then had to mount the steed. My mother and I rode this way twice. She instructed me that: "A woman should ride side-saddle. Riding with your legs apart is inelegant." Further-more, she told me that: "Riding a donkey is not like riding a horse. You can straddle a horse's middle, but have to perch upon a donkey's rear-end."

But, by then, it was no longer possible to ride a donkey along the route. During the war, fearing that their beasts would be commandeered by the military and taken away for good, the muleteers sold off their animals. This was all to the benefit of butchers and other folks who stewed the donkey meat and used the intestines as sausage skins. Not a shadow of a single donkey remained.

After sealing the deal with the coolie, Old Seven brought out a series of cloth-wrapped bundles prepared by my mother from the house. These he loaded one-by-one onto the rickshaw. I couldn't wait and had already climbed aboard while my mother was still dawdling on the step. She squatted in a curtsy to Old Zhang the doorkeeper and instructed: "You take care of our home. Sorry to give you so much grief." Old Zhang bowed in kind and bade my mother a safe journey.

Old Beijing folk had too much etiquette. I had a deep aversion to such complex rigmarole. I was anxious for Old Zhang to head indoors so that we could hasten away. Actually, Old Zhang and Old Seven didn't turn around and enter the courtyard until our rickshaw was out of sight. My mother explained that this was the custom for bidding farewell to people. The truth was that one should not turn one's back on a traveller before he had set off, lest he become an object of ridicule.

With two or three turns, the rickshaw reached the Eastern Gate. At that time, the Eastern Gate still had an arch above it. It looked magnificent. When people passed through the portal it boomed with echoes. I liked to shout once or twice and listen to my voice echoing back. That was enormous fun. Thinking of the elements that had disappeared from around the Eastern Gate and the donkeys that had gone to the pot, I wanted to imitate Second Head who shouted "Donkey meat! Fat and delicious!" in the alleyway. When I had belted out the word "donkey" my mother dabbed me with her palm and made me swallow what was about to come next. She scolded: "How can you – a girl – call out 'donkey meat!' in public?"

As a girl, there were so many things you were prohibited from doing.

Outside of the Eastern Gate stood a big square for drying out night-soil. All of the waste from the latrines in the east end of the city was dumped here to be desiccated. The place perpetually stank to high heaven, being festooned with flies and mosquitoes tussling away and laying eggs. And yet the land here was exceedingly fertile. Back then, the washrooms in Beijing were known as "privies". Usually located in the south-western corner of the courtyard, they consisted of a pit for squatting over without any flushing conduit. According to *Feng shui* theory, the south-western quadrant was the realm of malign spirits. The privy was felt to be the best weapon for banishing evil.

From the standpoint of modern architecture and anemology, the stench from a privy built like this would not be able to percolate into the centre of the courtyard. After three or five days, somebody would come over with a slender night-soil pail on his back and a long ladle to collect the slops. The service was performed by volunteers who never billed the householders. They would also clean the privy to boot. The gathered night-soil would be deposited outside the Eastern Gate, then dried and sold on as manure to those who required it. This business ought never to be looked down upon. It was a marvel that all of the night-soil from the east-end could come to be piled up on a single spot.

As time went by, someone monopolised this enterprise and became the local "Turd Baron". The Turd Barons were rich and powerful businessmen with gangland links. No one dared raise their hackles.

Passing through the manure square and turning to the north, the road gradually became rough. Both sides were lined with unmarked burial mounds. The mounds undulated and the road was pitted and bumpy. Some of the coffins were now exposed and had grown rotten and splintered so that, in broad daylight, everything within was on display. I would always turn my face and look, desirous to find anything peculiar beyond the skeletons. My mother tried to dissuade me, but I would insist on peeping. She would say that I was "a bold thief" and a "tomboy" rather than an ordinary girl. In actual fact, I just wanted to see if Sun Shun'er's bonny little lass was there. The father had carried the little box containing her body to the east. If he had deposited the bonny little lass down there, I now had the chance to check if the infant with the small white blotches on her head had survived intact.

The coolie complained about the bad terrain and expressed regret that he had taken on this job. My mother would then tip him again and again with extra coins. For my ma, this was part of her plan and she had factored these extras into her calculations. The coolie moaned that he would never come to this area again. He claimed that he might run into "a ghostly wall" on his way back.

Once, the coolie's wife's younger brother had passed over the graveyard outside the Eastern Gate. He wandered there the whole night, unable to escape from it. At daybreak, he saw that the ground was crosshatched all over with his own footprints. It transpired that he had been going round in circles all the while.

My mother reassured the coolie that by the time he had to turn back, the sun would still be high in the sky. When the sun is out, no ghosts dare reveal themselves. I blurted out that I was a ghost and I was outside now. With these words, I pulled a cross-eyed expression. The coolie turned his head and shot me a glare, then snorted with laughter.

Before the sun had reached its zenith, we arrived at Sun Palace. The coolie paused at the entrance to the village and refused to carry on, whining about how rough the surface of the road was and how he despaired over having to put his rickshaw through such an ordeal. He said that when we arranged to hire him, we only told him we wanted to go to Sun Palace and didn't mention which particular household we planned to visit. My mother and I had to climb off the rickshaw and tramp towards the village carrying parcels of assorted size.

The surname of the family we had come to see was Cao. I called the lady of the house Second Aunt and her husband Second Uncle. My mother had no sisters and in the slang of today this auntie would be her "bosom buddy". When she was a girl in South Camp outside Chaoyang Gate they were both seamstresses in the same workshop, picking out a living with a needle. In short, sisters made through adversity. Later, she married Cao Dada, a market gardener, and my mother married my father, a teacher.

From then on, the two women's lives diverged completely. My mother was the second wife of my widowed father and found herself the spouse of a professor. My Second Aunt became a village bride, raising sheep and working the land. The lady and the village wife were of common cultural stock, being unlettered women. The only difference was that my mother could scrawl her name – Chen Maizhen. That was my father's contribution. Second Aunt went to the grave unable to write her own signature. When important occasions came around, she would impress an inky mark with her index finger. This was far less complicated than assembling a name one separate stroke at a time.

Second Aunt had a son who was born in Sun Palace village. His adopted name was Solar Cao and Second Uncle bemoaned how this name was too grand, too unwieldy, and too fulsome. So, he gave him the nickname "Sunny". All of the villagers called him Sunny as they found that it tripped off the tongue easily. Few of them knew his official name. Sunny adored painting. I showed his picture of a cockscomb to my father and he said that it was a pity Solar Cao was raised in Sun Palace.

"The sun, of course, should make his home in Sun Palace," I reasoned.

"The sun lives in the Eastern Sea, perched upon a tree called the Chinese hibiscus," my father added.

"The sun is a big fireball. If the fire fell on a tree it would scorch the tree to death."

"The perching sun is a three-legged crow."

I couldn't always understand him. "Do you know the story about the archer Hou Yi shooting down the suns?"

my father enquired. "Ten suns once shone together in the sky. They made the land dry and barren. Not even a single blade of grass could survive. Hou Yi was a crack shot. He felled each sun one-by-one. Upon impact, each let out a sound like gold ingots cracking. When they landed on the earth they turned into three-legged crows."

I asked why the crows had three legs. My father informed me that the sun belongs to the element of *yang*. Odd numbers are considered to be *yang*, so that is why the birds have three legs. When I grew up, I had the opportunity to inspect the paintings on silk unearthed from the Mawangdui archaeological site in Henan Province. These featured tripedal crows, representing the sun. They were casting their light on an old lady with a walking stick. I also noticed the same birds in the frescoes in Beijing Airport, standing within bright gold circles. When I caught sight of them, I felt a twinge of gratitude to Hou Yi; thankful that he didn't exterminate all the crows and thought to leave one for us. Otherwise, there would be no sun in the sky and people would not survive.

Before we entered the village, the big yellow dog belonging to the Cao family galloped out from the roadside vegetable plot. It overtook my mother and darted directly towards me. It reared up on its hind legs, pressing its front paws into my chest. I would have been floored if I hadn't been so tall. I bellowed: "Go away!"

The yellow dog wagged its tail and refused to go. I stroked its head and found that many grass seeds had become tangled in its coat.

After all, it was autumn.

"A whole year has passed and the yellow dog still recognises you," my mother commented.

"Of course. We are sisters like you and my Second Aunt."

"Aren't you ashamed to lower yourself to the level of an animal?"

"This is nothing. The lady in Auntie Wang's home calls her dog her son."

The Cao family's yellow dog had erect ears, an upturned tail, and four chubby paws. It possessed the fine bearing of a canine. A modern pet store would give him a nice academic name like "Chinese field dog". But it was just a common, worthless local mutt. In my eyes though, the mongrel was as noble as a famous hound. It was humane by nature, owning its own dignity and emotions and having more candour and passion than many a man. My deep lifelong love of dogs began with this yellow one.

The yellow dog ran in front of us in a sycophantic fashion. Now and then, he would turn his head and look at us. My mother and I followed on behind. My mother said: "This dog is lovely."

"Just like me."

"How could the yellow dog know that we were coming today?"

"It can smell us a mile off," I answered.

The yellow dog went home to pass on the message and the members of the Cao family came out to greet us.

Chapter Three:
The Yellow Dog, the Thick Porridge, and the Buddha's Hand Melon

The Caos were pleasantly surprised at our coming, even though we had caught them unprepared. The whole family had been eating their meal under the gourd trellis. They plonked down their bowls and hurried to the door.

Second Aunt tugged my mother's arms constantly and repeated: "You should have given us the message sooner so Sunny's pa could have met you with a cart at the village entrance."

"City folk aren't used to walking on country tracks," Second Uncle said. "The road is muddy."

I hadn't seen them for a whole year. I found that my short and stout Second Aunt had become brawnier. She had small eyes and a big mouth, as per a plain woman. Second Uncle was straight-backed and had big eyes and a small mouth, as per a handsome man. Their voices had a touch of east end rhotacism and burr. This brought to mind Beijing pork cakes from the east and made one feel on relaxed, intimate terms. Even if you had only met them for the first time, you felt you had known them for eight hundred years.

The Cao family's table was arrayed with corn buns, thick porridge, and several bowls of cowpeas. In the middle was a ceramic jar containing pickled Buddha's hand melons. The fare was simple and unadorned – their ordinary food.

Sunny carried over two small stools and was all smiles. He ladled out two bowls of porridge and laid out two pairs of chopsticks. He fumbled out a couple of salted duck eggs from a jar. It was a special treat for the guests. I could see that my arrival had delighted him. His dog-like front teeth were exposed as he wiped the small stools again and again with his hands. I was compelled to call him "elder brother" because he was my senior.

All the local farmers grew vegetables. People would come over to buy and collect them early in the morning before heaving their carrying poles back to the city to begin selling. Every resident of the capital knew that Sun Palace was the renowned market garden of Beijing.

The most famous fresh produce from Sun Palace were the Chinese chives and green leeks. Chinese chives were a market staple between spring and autumn. They measured one span (from the thumb to the index finger) and had purple roots, hence their nickname "pheasant's neck". I knew that the rebel leader Huang Chao wrote in one of his poems of how a "sky surging fragrance permeates all over Chang'an". Old Huang was talking about chrysanthemums, but I loved to use this line to describe the pheasant's neck. In the city, when one family was eating pheasant's neck, the whole lane would smell it. The fragrance really did surge. Green leeks were a kind of fresh produce that appeared during winter in the run up to Spring Festival. They issued from the greenhouses at Sun Palace. The tender green leek was no thicker than a strand of hair, and was yellowish jade. Wontons made from them were an irreplaceable winter delicacy.

When Second Uncle occasionally came to shop for Spring Festival, he would bring us a small bunch of green leeks. Second Aunt would wrap them in cotton wadding to prevent them from freezing. Green leeks were always used for making wontons together with the meat from a piglet's forelegs, fresh shards of ginger and chicken broth. One bite of it would make you so happy that you wanted to spin a cartwheel. However, the green leek wontons were made so our parents could eat their fill, while kids were only permitted a nibble. That was something rare. Our chef, Old Wang, would say "these are wasted on you sprogs".

The Buddha's hand melon in the ceramic jar was pickled on the spot by the Caos themselves. They were plucked in the fields and slipped into the container straightaway. A few grains of sea salt would be added before they were eaten. Using this method, the fruit would have a salty tang without losing its original texture. To use modern terminology, the "eco-texture of the food was preserved". Of course, only fresh produce was suitable for spontaneous pickling. Withered and dried-up specimens had to be brined for longer. The Buddha's hand melon in the jar was complemented by red peppers and verdigris garlic cloves, which stirred up diner's appetites. I pinched one piece, cocked back my head and dropped it into my gaping mouth. It crackled on my tongue. So delicious. My mother shot me a disapproving stare. I was undaunted. Once we entered Sun Palace all her rules became obsolete.

Here, I persisted in my old way of doing things. Here, everyone was their own master. When I saw that the adults had no intention of sitting at the table, I pinched another morsel and chewed it in an exaggerated way. Nowadays, I think the Buddha's hand melon is rather fascinating. It used to thrive but has now become something of an endangered species in the markets. All those who sold vegetables from a cart once had a basket of them. They were more slender than a gourd, yet had greater girth than a cucumber. They were white on the outside and had pale flesh too. The skin was thick and the seeds tough. The fruit had no taste. The great advantage was that it was cheap and easy to store. Ordinary people took them as a mainstay. Kids in the alleys of Beijing soon became fed up of them. In summer, they would have them at every meal with no other kind of vegetable. How many children of today have even seen them? Where did all these country bumpkin melons go? I miss them.

With the arrival of my mother and me, a ham hock from the Heavenly-Blessed Store and sesame cakes materialised on the table. We asked Old Seven to go to the West Four Archway and buy the marinated ham hock specially. The cakes had been baked by Uncle Liu the night before. These were the necessities we were certain to bring with us on every visit. With these two additions, the dining table in the farming household immediately became sumptuous and boisterous. Sandwiching the pork into a cake, I could polish off two in one sitting. At that point, my mother indicated that I should drink only porridge and save the cakes for Sunny to eat. Second Aunt and Second Uncle were never stingy or proper when it came to eating. They would wedge mighty chunks of meat into their mouths and let the grease ooze out and coat their hands. Watching their behaviour at the table made one feel very cozy and content in return.

Sunny's chopsticks seemed to have eyes. They gravitated towards the fattiest meat. He would gorge himself from his bowl while fixating on the plate. Second Uncle said: "Not even during Spring Festival can we lay our hands on such a choice marinated ham hock. This bests our craving for good food."

"Sunny's big aunt thinks he's in want of a decent feed," Second Aunt commented. "Every time she comes she brings delicious things with her. If it's not marinated ham hock, it's fried mutton. What makes an auntie a true auntie? That is a true auntie."

Under the assault of the entire Cao family, the majority of the huge ham hock vanished in no time at all. My mother said that half should be kept for tomorrow for *a narrow river runs a longer course*. Second Aunt responded: "No need to save it. If we are going to eat, we should just demolish it now. We only have such a fine treat once a year."

Second Uncle agreed with Second Auntie. He picked up a large globule of the quivering, bright red pork skin. Sunny's chopsticks flayed a hefty portion from the bone. The whole family ate without any inhibitions. They feasted joyfully and with contentment.

Above their heads, the cicadas sang without tiring. Nobody cared when the insects' thin urine floated down into their porridge bowls. The fruits of the gourd vine overhead had reached the size of teacups and had fine down on their skin, which shivered gently in the wind. I don't know when exactly it appeared, but the yellow dog stole over quietly. It nudged my leg, its tail wagging merrily. I knew what was on its mind. It knew what was on my mind too. I wasn't fazed by my mother spotting me picking up a piece of meat that had both fat and lean. I dared not give the animal it all at once. I concealed it in my palm and the yellow dog understood me tacitly. It nudged open my hand beneath the table and gulped down the meat without a sound before licking my hand. At last, that yellow head rested on my knee. It didn't look at the meat, but trained its dark eyes on me, waiting for a reward.

Second Aunt kicked the dog, saying: "He puts on a lovely show for guests. Give him an inch and he'll take a yard."

I loved the Cao family's thick porridge, stewed in a colossal wok. The cracked corn was of the larger grain size and chewing it was a pleasant sensation. Red and yellow in colour, owing to the addition of beans, the aroma wafted into the courtyard as soon as the lid was removed from the pan. That was the scent of grain. Every time I smelled it, I felt satisfied and touched. This was the essence of life. Marinated ham hock was, after all, something showy and rootless and fitful. I knew a veteran practitioner of Chinese medicine by the name of Peng Yutang. He once observed that: "Fatty and greasy meat causes mucous, so one should refrain from eating too much hock. It can make adults susceptible to phlegm-induced syncope and dizziness. Children's heart spirits are prone to becoming clouded with excess phlegm. These are all difficult diseases to cure."

We owned a walking stick that had been passed down from our ancestors. It was decorated with characters saying, *a cloth gown is snug, vegetable roots are scrumptious, books and poetry have a lingering aftertaste*. I have no special memory about the dress and the books, but vegetables remain permanently lodged in my mind. Oh, the human race. We can never forget to eat.

I never drank such sweet porridge from such a huge wok anywhere else but Sun Palace.

After the meal, the dishes and plates were all piled on the table. Second Aunt didn't want to wash them, nor did Second Uncle. Naturally, Sunny thought that it was not his responsibility either. Everybody was in a sluggish state. This made me think of the expression, *black bears won't play with a pitchfork when they are bloated*. This refers to circus skits involving a black bear playing with a farm tool. Before the performance, the creature was refused any food because, with a full stomach, he would only crouch down and refuse to listen to his master's commands.

Such a situation was forbidden in our household. As soon as we laid aside our chopsticks, my mother would instruct me to carry the dishes and plates to the kitchen, wash them and arrange them according to the right categories. My mother thought this was a girl's duty. She should not have to be urged, but do it voluntarily. In the future, should a young married woman become lazy and sluggish after having had enough to eat, people would laugh at her. At this time though, nobody in the Cao family would laugh at you. Everything seemed to proceed naturally, and the whole family did as they pleased. Great! Why should folks be so hard on themselves?

Apart from the marinated ham hock, my mother brought some of my brothers' hand-me-down clothes for Sunny. Sunny was quiet in company, but his eyes shone brightly. Second Aunt said: "Sunny's spirit and guts are all in his eyes." His eyes were filled with so many things, like trees, people and colourful clouds. Whatever he wanted, he would take from his eyes and paint on paper.

Second Aunt praised the worn-out clothes as she lauded Sunny's eyes, commenting that: "When Sunny wears your brothers' clothes, nobody will be able to tell him apart from the city folk. Nobody will be able to tell that he is a vegetable planter from Sun Palace." My mother agreed: "That's true. Sunny has a good aspect. He's bound to do something great when he grows up. He might be an office clerk."

In my mother's eyes, office clerk was an extremely important position. My father once held that role for a few days before he was accepted as a teacher at the National Peking Arts College. My mother believed it was a very decent occupation. It was not a position that everybody could obtain. Cultivated in this way, I was determined from an early age that I should one day become an office clerk. During the Cultural Revolution, factories sent personnel to the countryside to recruit workers. I asked if they were recruiting office clerks. They told me that they were only taking on workers. I answered that I wanted to be an office clerk. The recruiters declared that: "Workers are great. The labouring class takes the lead in everything. Once you have entered the factory you will understand that. Workers have work uniforms, labour insurance, and two bars of soap every month, but an office clerk receives nothing."

Sunny showed no interest in my brothers' clothes. What he was interested in was a sheaf of scrap paper that I'd brought for him. I had collected these bits of paper in the course of everyday life, including wrapping paper from tea, medicines and face cream, and half-used notebooks. Sunny needed the scraps to paint on. He sketched gourds, miniature temples, and crickets. Anything could be his subject, even the yellow dog. Sunny would lay out his canvasses with great care under the mat on top of the *kang*. Only when he had completely filled one sheet would he move on to the next, never allowing any wastage.

I mentioned that my seventh older brother was a keen painter too. Officially, he worshipped the great master painter Xu Beihong as his teacher. Old Seven also painted gourds and crickets. Sunny said that he wished he had a brother who could paint. It was a pity that he hadn't. I promised that if the chance arose I would introduce Sunny to him. He was happy to hear this and asked many questions about Old Seven's painting, wishing that he might have the opportunity to meet him. It dawned on me that in Sunny's mind Old Seven had already been enshrined as a god.

Chapter Four:
The Kiln Pit, the Small Fish,
and Tomatoes

After the meal, without Second Auntie having to issue an order, Sunny knew what he had to do next. He took down the fish basket from the wall, picked up a splintered straw hat and put it on his head. Noticing what he was doing, I immediately piped up that I wanted to go too. Second Auntie warned that in the sticks the sun was too fierce and we should take care not to get sunstroke. I told her that I wasn't deterred.

"Let her go," my mother insisted. "Every time we come here she ends up looking like a broiled red shrimp anyway."

"Your family is bound to complain when they see their clean, white girl tanned as dark as Duke Bao," Second Auntie replied.

"I won't moan," I said. "I'm perfectly willing."

I followed Sunny out of the village and headed due south. Sunny placed his straw hat on my head. It was too big and covered my eyes so I could only see the ground beneath my feet. Once we had crawled our way into the cornfields, the leaves of the corn scratched bloody tracks along my arms. It stung. Sunny was by now already out of sight. The yellow dog overtook me. Left alone, I felt sealed in, suffocating. The crops were all taller than me and I could not escape from the canes that encircled me. I felt like I'd run into a ghostly wall. I pleaded for help from the yellow dog, shouting: "Big Yellow! Big Yellow!" My voice was already inflected with weeping. To the south, the mutt barked. I fumbled in the direction of his call and soon gave the ghostly wall the slip.

Sunny and the yellow dog were waiting for me at the edge of the field. I appeared before them in a sorry plight. My face was drenched with sweat and my body riddled with scratches. I didn't know where my straw hat had gone. Sunny ordered the yellow dog to go back and sniff it out. Once more, the hound inched back into the cornfield and re-emerged with the headgear in its mouth. The hamlet in front of us was the Xia Family Garden. Beside the small settlement was a pond thick with lotus leaves. The local people called it the Kiln Pit on account of it being formed from the hollow once used for digging clay for tiles. Water and pondweed had now reclaimed the site. The surface of the pool was quiet, smooth and free from ripples. The depth was unfathomable. When people waded in, the waters would lap against their shins one moment and then overwhelm their heads the next. Folks would always hear tell of kids who went out for fun and ended up being drowned in the Kiln Pit outside of the Eastern Gate. For that reason, it was a place of foreboding and few young-sters dared paddle there.

If a mother got wind that her children had been playing there, there would be no escaping a good thrashing, no matter where they hid. Little Four from Paoju Alley near my home went out to play in the Kiln Pit and perished. When he was carried back, they laid his body in a corner near the entrance to the alley, shrouded in a mat, his hands and feet still poking out; swollen, purplish and terrifying to behold. I rushed over to take a peek before recoiling immediately.

The indigo-grey feet gave me nightmares the whole night long and the face shielded by the cracked straw mat allowed people's fancies to run wild.

City kids' complexions would turn sallow when they spoke of the Kiln Pit. To them, it held more fear than a loping tiger.

Sunny was going to the Kiln Pit to tickle tiddlers. The idea of him going in the water made me very upset. Trailing behind him, I was both afraid and hopeful. I kept on murmuring: "Can you do it? Can you?"

I was desperate to eat the fish, but worried about him drowning.

Sunny patted his wicker creel and said: "Later when you see this, you will know whether I've been successful or not."

On the bank of the Kiln Pit, Sunny peeled off his clothes and dived into the water. It was so clear that I could see his legs kicking beneath the surface. Sunny told me that he was treading water and that his side of the pool seemed bottomless. He pointed eastward and said: "The water over there is shallow. The sun shines on that part. It's warmer, so there are more fish to be had." Maybe the water on that side of the pit was not in fact as deep. When Sunny dived into it, silt was whipped up to the top. Sometimes when he dived in, however, he would not resurface for a long time. I was petrified that he might pitch headlong into the sludge and become stuck fast. I shouted vigorously from the bank and the yellow dog joined in. Sunny raised his head out of the water and barked: "What are you shouting at? You've scared the fish away. Don't stir up trouble here. Just go and find a cool spot to rest."

"I must keep an eye on you at all times. If you drown it'll be me who has to break the news to your folks."

"I won't drown," Sunny was resolute. "I was born in the Year of the Dragon. I'm the second grandpa of the God of the Sea."

I strolled around the Kiln Pit while Sunny was catching fish. The Xia Family Garden was surrounded by vegetable plots. The veggies were far superior to those at Sun Palace. It was closer to the East and West Dam River. In the Yuan Dynasty, this waterway was a transportation hub linked to the capital. Thus, the water table was constant and the land fertile. All the vegetables cultivated here were fresh and succulent.

On top of that, I knew that to the northwest of Sun Palace and the Xia Family Garden there was a place called the Land of Border Peonies. I had been longing to visit it and was eager for Sunny to accompany me so I could see them in full bloom. Sunny informed me that peonies flowered in spring and now it was already autumn. The only blossoms would be those of the bristle grass. Second Uncle said: "The Land of the Border Peonies is ideal for vegetables too. There are no peonies over there, though the market gardener Old Zhao grew the odd one in his courtyard. By a stretch of their imagination, some men of letters concocted the name we use today."

"How can the Land of Border Peonies be compared with Sun Palace?" asked Second Aunt. "Remember how special and grand Sun Palace once was."

What I hadn't expected was that several dozen years later the Land of Border Peonies, which had been falsely named, would become a major station on the Beijing City Metro. It mushroomed into a prosperous and lively community. Some worldly matters prove extremely hard to predict.

A stone tablet stood among the grasses to the east of the

Kiln Pit. To my surprise, I chanced upon a few tomatoes there. At that time, tomatoes were a rarity. The vegetable hawkers who went along the streets with a carrying-pole would shout: "Coriander, celery, spicy peppers, aubergines, lentils, tender garlic shoots." But there would be no tomatoes among them. Tomatoes appeared very belatedly on the tables of ordinary folk. Back then, tomatoes occasionally flashed before kids' faces. They were red, round, juicy and costly; eaten as a fruit. Those scant tomatoes by the stone tablet were overripe. Their complexion had turned to mauve. Seductive and garish, they were impossible to resist. I padded over and pinched one from the vine without hesitation. When it comes to things which grow in the open fields, it is hard to tell who the owner is. I squinted around and no eyes were staring at me, save for those of the yellow dog who lapped up my surreptitious behaviour. I questioned the hound: "Should we nab them or not?"

The yellow dog wagged its tail in merry agreement. Then, impolitely, I plucked off a bigger one and popped it into the fold of my dress. I was thinking about retrieving an even more glorious specimen so that I could take the lot back and have a proper feast. Unfortunately, my way was blocked by the stone tablet. When I studied the characters on its surface, I didn't recognise most of them. I could only decipher a handful of words, namely "Your highness … Xia …" So, I intoned to the grave tablet: "Grandpa Xia, I am going to eat a few of your tomatoes. I can't help myself. I'm a gannet."

Of course, nobody cared about what I was doing. Only the insects chirped away in their lairs among the tufts of grass.

After giving my greeting, I sidled up to the Kiln Pit without difficulty. Sunny's basket was now teeming with fish. They were all the size of ears of wheat. Mixed in among them were tiny restless eels.

When Sunny saw the tomatoes in my hands, he gasped: "How dare you lay your mitts on Second Xia's tomatoes? The Xia family has been keeping them for seed. Second Xia will batter you to death with a spade."

"I'm not afraid of Second Xia. I'm not even afraid of the ghosts in the Lama Temple."

I knew that Sunny had been longing to encounter the ghosts at the Lama Temple. He mentioned more than once that he wanted to tag along with me to see how they shooed away the spirits. The Ghost Shooing Ceremony was held in January. Other than when they were selling green leeks to us, the Cao family were nervous about coming to our home. They were reluctant to meet my father as they worried that he might give them the cold shoulder. In reality, my father never spoke a word about these "relatives" in the countryside. He neither blew hot nor cold where they were concerned. He was a teacher and that was mostly their way. He would make others feel that there was a barrier between them.

Suddenly, Sunny pointed behind me and yelled: "Second Xia is coming!"

I took to my heels with Sunny behind me. The yellow dog had already run out of sight.

We bounced over canals, ran through pumpkin fields, dashed through forests of willows and navigated thorn bushes. I tore all the way, fearful of looking back.

When we reached Sun Palace, I discovered that there was no Second Xia in pursuit. It was all Sunny's fabrication. I complained at having been cheated by him. Sunny grinned, exposing his wonky canines, and reminded me:

"You told me that you weren't afraid of Second Xia. If you aren't afraid of him, why did you run?"

"Wasn't I the one who stole his tomatoes?"

Sunny took my hand and led me home with the fish basket on his back. I raised my head and saw how bewitching and emotive the sunset in the west was. I pointed out that it was fit to paint. Sunny noted how the clouds were crimson. Tomorrow was bound to be a clear day. This spell of early autumn hot weather would be over within a matter of days.

Second Aunt greeted Sunny at the door and commanded him to help her mend the kitchen fire and do the cooking.

Chapter Five:
The Milky Way, the Weasel,
and the Tobacco Pipe

Dinner that night was a particular highlight for the Cao family – baked cake with small stewed fish.

The fish were those little ears of wheat Sunny had caught from the Xia Family Garden. A giant wok, a wood fire and bellows with a short stool were all that was needed. Sunny busied himself adding more firewood and pumping the bellows in the kitchen. Everything was spic and span and before long the water in the wok came to the boil. Second Aunt tipped the prepared fish into the pan, added a ladleful of homemade sauce and tossed in a bundle of green leeks and two cloves of garlic. She stirred them slowly. Second Uncle grasped a handful of cornmeal dough and patted it into a succession of cakes, lining the rim of the wok. Among the rising steam the unbaked dough resembled kids hand-in-hand, motionless and delectable. Next, the broad cover of the wok was placed on top to create a tight seal. When the steam above the cover burst into full bloom, Sunny retrieved the largest piece of firewood from the stove so that the blaze eavened out and became gentler. The fish stewed over the moderate fire. The whole family cooperated in perfect synchrony as if staging a performance. Each member had his or her role and duty. How wonderful!

The sweet scent of the fish and the cake drifted out from the wok, making our chests tighten with expectation. I neither wanted to sit nor stand. I simply wanted to go over to the pan and remove the cover to see what was happening inside. On the dining table were tender cucumbers with their prickles still intact and miniature water radishes which would dribble out moisture when bitten. Added to that, the ram's horn onions were sweet rather than acidic. All these were meant to be dipped in simple condiments made out of soya beans, sun-dried the whole summer long. Bubbles clumped on the surface the moment the jar was opened, indicating that it was fermented to a tee.

Second Aunt sliced my tomatoes as if she were quartering a watermelon. She dropped the pieces into a rough bowl and put it directly in front of me. The tomato seeds were flinty and had to be spat out. The flesh, meanwhile, had dried out and was no longer piquant. The chore of spitting pips while eating seemed to be my thief's comeuppance. When I thought about it, it didn't feel worthwhile.

The cakes and the fish were ready and had to be taken out of the wok at the same time. The setting sun shone on the table so that the golden cakes mingled with the light and formed a congenial and touching scene. They looked like something otherworldly deposited here among men. I was too excited. The barbs of the small fish had become brittle and would not jag the eater's mouth. The flesh stewed in the sauce had acquired flavour and delicacy. On popping one in, you could first savour the soup then nibble the meat. What fine stuff!

In later years, I have been to many places and consumed numerous kinds of fish – fried, steamed, boiled, stewed and raw. None were as flavoursome as the fish and cakes at Sun Palace. Eaten once but remembered for a lifetime.

That evening, I chomped down a lot. My stomach was

filled with at least twenty bodies of those ears of wheat. I swore off the heads in case they organised an uprising in my belly and started to bite back. If that happened, how could I be any sort of match for them? As for the cakes, I only ate the crusts. They were treacly and crisp and produced a crunching sound when chewed. I couldn't keep my hands off them. Sunny voluntarily made do with the innards I left behind.

The yellow dog crept in from afar. It glanced at us from time to time, sporting a wronged look. I asked Second Aunt why they didn't feed the yellow dog. She explained that dogs in the countryside had to forage for themselves. I felt a tug of sorrow for that yellow dog. It was so loyal and yet didn't receive a single mouthful in return. If I were the dog, I wouldn't be my playmate anymore.

After dinner, Second Aunt and my mother sat chatting in the courtyard. They always seemed to have an endless supply of topics. Second Uncle perched alongside them silently smoking one pipeful after another. The basket of tobacco stood by his feet and he stroked some shag while he puffed away. The leaves had been cultivated on the family's plot and harvested and dried. They sheared them into slivers and then rubbed them by hand. The smoke was heady and spicy and caused others to gag. Second Uncle saw that I was interested in the tobacco. He knocked his pipe and said: "In the future, you girls should learn how to smoke too. When you smoke, your body absorbs the scent of tobacco oil so you can save a lot of fuss. Ground beetles, scorpions and centipedes won't care to go near you."

I said that I didn't want to risk smoking and nor did my brothers. They were scared of my father, who was averse to the habit. Once, Old Three was discovered taking a secret drag in the lavatory and was dealt a brisk hiding. His buttocks were so swollen that he couldn't sit on a stool. He grimaced in pain. Old Two had to dab half a bottle of turpentine onto the sore spot.

"That's how it is in your home," Second Uncle observed. "Your family has too many rules. Here, even a snake can become addicted. Second Xia's grandpa over at the Xia Family Garden smoked all his life. Of course, that was opium. Every day he would lie on the *kang*, riding the clouds and mounting the mists until he smoked the household to the dogs. The second day after he died, a long black snake fell from the beam of the house and lay still and outstretched on the coffin lid. Someone said that snakes are the guardians of the home. The black snake was loath to be parted from him. It was so overcome with grief that it keeled over. In actual fact, whenever the old man had smoked opium on the *kang*, the serpent up on the beam had inhaled the smoke too. As time went by, it became hooked as well, so when the old man died and no more opium was to be had, the snake up above was hit by cravings and couldn't stand it anymore."

I was keen to know what had happened to Second Xia's family snake after that. Second Uncle admitted he had no idea and didn't try to follow it up. My mother interjected, saying: "This girl's never satisfied until she's gotten to the bottom of everything. Sometimes her questions are bizarre."

Second Aunt recalled that the old man in the Xia family had been gone more than twenty years. Who would still be able to remember the snake?

Second Uncle stuffed his pipe and handed it to my mother. My mother accepted it and skilfully sucked the flame from Second Aunt's hands. She puffed gently through her mouth. I never imagined that my mother might do that and had never seen her so much as touch a cigarette at home. Now that we had come to Sun Palace, she was heaving on a pipe. She was quite open and free here. I thought that I must tell my father when I got home.

Second Aunt asked Second Uncle if he had fed the sheep. He replied that late last night he had flung two baskets of grass into the fold. This morning when the sun came out, he led them from the pen and tethered them outside the village. When he came back, their stomachs were fit to burst. Second Aunt told my mother: "The sheep at Sun Palace have to be fed in the fold because all the surrounding fields are given over to vegetables. If they mow down any old neighbour's crops, it would cause a stink. They're now middling-sized and we bought them from a dealer outside Desheng Gate. By the end of the year they'll be at their best to be slaughtered. Then we will send you mutton."

I immediately thought about mutton and carrot dumplings. Inhaling deeply, I could almost smell the pungent aroma of the meat.

Sunny was weaving a basket from limber tree twigs. It was getting dark. There were no electric bulbs in the countryside. They didn't light an oil lamp either. In the dim light, people could fuzzily make things out. Sunny boasted that, even when it was pitch black, he could still manage to weave a basket. Basket-making required dexterity of touch, but not one's eyes. Sunny invited me to guess what type of basket he was working on now. I surmised that it must be a round one with a handle like the one behind the house that they stored scythed grass in. Sunny retorted that I was wrong. His basket would be shaped like an ingot; both ends curved with the middle portion slim. This kind of basket was for a girl. I guessed that Sunny must be creating it for me. I began to ponder what use I would have for it in the city. Eventually, I decided it could make a good nest for our spotted cat. That way she would not always creep under my quilt.

Second Uncle was going out to man the shelter in the field. He had grown half a *mu* of sweet melons. He was not worried about thieves lifting the nearly-ripe fruit, but about animals on the prowl. Second Uncle left with his clothes under his arm and the yellow dog in tow. The dog was a key component of the evening guard. I scanned about outside through the fence slats. The fields were completely black. In the distance, fireflies jammed together like regaling fairies. A pair of green eyes flashed by in the darkness. I slid nearer to my mother, unperturbed by the peculiar reek of smoke that clung to her body. Second Uncle yelped: "That thing running over there is a weasel. It has its mind on the chicks behind the house."

Sunny protested that he had jammed the coop door shut with a stone. The weasel's little paws wouldn't be able to budge it.

Second Aunt referred to this small countryside animal by its nickname "yellow wolf". Sunny used its official name, weasel, just as some people called him Sunny and others Solar Cao. I quizzed him on what a yellow wolf looked like. Were they like the paintings of grey wolves in books? Sunny remarked that a weasel is rangy and thin, in excess of a yard in length. It had the talent of being able to make its bones shrink so it could squeeze through the smallest of holes. It was a master at rustling chickens. I implored him to catch me a few to inspect. Sunny said: "A few? I couldn't even lay my hands on one. That is a cunning, sly creature. It's got the air of a ghost. Folks shouldn't provoke them."

Sunny went on to tell me that one night when he was returning from the melon field, the moonlight was so intense that he could even make out the clods and particles of earth on the road. Suddenly, he saw a weasel standing erect on the road, waving its paws and dancing for the moon. Sunny asked me if I knew what it was doing.

I replied that I didn't. How could I know anything about weasels' business?

Sunny explained that it was worshipping the moon. Why, I wanted to know, should it do that? He disclosed that, like a fox, when weasels come of age they are transfigured into spectres. They practise self-conditioning until they are ready to make the desired change. They can transform themselves into an enchantress or an old codger. However, a weasel is somewhat inferior to a fox in its aptitude for self-conditioning. A fox may attempt to make its own immortality pills, but a weasel cannot.

I was adamant that he ought to have been able to bag the weasel that night like he did the fish.

"How could I? Before I had the chance to get near it, it sneezed and said *peep-pee-pee – bad luck*. I shouldn't have come out that night."

I asked why.

"I interrupted his business. It needed an extra five hundred years to perfect its self-conditioning."

What a pitiful weasel.

A gentle cool breeze drew in from the west. The leaves on the trees did not move, nor did the grass. Yet I sensed it. To the west was the Swallow Mountain, known as the Western Mountain by Beijing people. The mountain lay straight across the horizon like a huge dragon. I looked towards the south and could not make out the Western Mountain. The lights in the sky in the distance were the lamps in the city. I looked straight above my head. The sky was honeycombed with stars. The constellations of the cowherd and girl weaver gazed at each other from aeons away. The two kids carried in the cowherd's basket sparkled brightly. The entire Milky Way was immense and magnificent. Faint as it was, it bristled with light and still spanned the entire firmament. People were touched with melancholy when they thought about that vast river separating the cowherd from his family. The mother and offspring were fated never to meet.

Second Auntie reflected: "Girl, you're looking at the Milky Way. I'll let you in on a secret. You must remember the old ditty: *When the Milky Way alters its stance, folks should wear cotton clothes and pants. When the Milky Way forms two prongs, folk should put much less on.* You should know about this for when you become a mother. You should consult the heavens to know what the youngsters should wear and when. Let the Milky Way be your guide."

I probed Second Auntie about what is meant by *alters its stance*. She explained that it was when it adjusted its direction. For example, at the moment it stretched from the north to the south, so this was summer time. Once it shifted, we had to put on thick coats. I questioned whether it was adjusting its direction right now or else forming a fork. Second Auntie hummed and hawed for some time before saying it could be that it was in fact adjusting its direction.

Actually, Second Auntie was unclear about the matter.

The chirruping of the autumn insects in the meadows was brazen enough to rouse the deaf. It seemed that the whole world was abuzz with their tune. Each insect was trying its best to showcase its fine throat, proclaiming its existence out loud. The poultry-hungry, ever-exercising weasel was among them. In the depth of night they added vitality, inspiration, trickiness, and uncertainty to the hinterlands of Sun Palace. I told Sunny that he ought to take me to see the Sun Palace tomorrow.

"Is there anything of interest to see?" was Sunny's response. "It's just a tumbledown temple on its last legs."

"When all is said and done, that tumbledown temple is still a palace. This is the only place beyond the Eastern Gate that's been given that name."

"Isn't the Lama Temple a palace?"

"The Lama Temple is within the city limits. It's inside Anding Gate."

"If I take you to the Sun Palace you must take me to the Lama Temple. I want to see how they drive away ghosts."

I assured him straightaway, saying "no problem".

The year before last, I followed my father to the Lama Temple twice to witness how they practised exorcism. I passed on the details to an expectant Sunny, who hoped every day that his chance to visit the place would come around. The emperors of the Qing Dynasty believed in Tantric Buddhism and the Lama Temple was formerly the royal residence of the Emperor Yongzheng. Every January, the Ghost Shooing Ceremony was an occasion of great importance in Beijing. The temple would begin its preparations far in advance and the Emperor would deploy inspectors to oversee the event. The emperors may have been banished with the founding of the Republic of China, but the ceremony remained a grand spectacle unchanged in spite of the new era. Whether there was a monarch or not, the aspirations of the city masses stayed constant, namely to be contented and drive away disasters.

Old Zhang, our family's doorkeeper, obdurately believed in the deity of the Lama Temple. He frequently went there to burn incense and to seek counsel. Even when a tiny boil erupted on his face he would go over and enquire if he should pop it or not. It was a relief to us that the Lama Temple was not far away. We lived on Theatre Stage Lane and the Lama Temple stood at the entrance to it. It was just a few strides away. You could run there and back before a batch of dumplings was fully steamed. Once Old Zhang twisted his ankle and it became swollen. Our cook Old Wang ribbed him with the question: "Shall we go to the hospital or the Lama Temple?"

On the day of the ceremony, a stage was constructed in front of the Hall of the Heavenly King. The platform was mantled in red carpet and the area below was a sea of spectators' heads. Even the wind could not cut through them. Thousands and thousands of people waited in silence for the opening ceremony. When the time came, the melee of gongs, drums and bugles shook the heavens. First of all, the Four Great Heavenly Kings appeared in their gold helmets and armour. They were solemn in their grandeur and, following their dance, they occupied the corners of the quadrangle. Then, a troupe of lively and mischievous children bounded and bounced with joy, enchanting the onlookers. Next, when the drums changed their tone, a white ghostly manifestation appeared on the stage. He wore a skeletal mask and waved a recruitment card in his hand. It was ghastly and bloodcurdling to behold. The pale ghost drew quite close to the audience. He cast around white powder as he patrolled. To be doused in that powder was a sign of misfortune. All the onlookers recoiled, leaving the square denuded. The old hands would not press to the front, instead removing themselves safely to the rear of the crowd.

After the ghost performed his turn, the Buddha's warrior attendant took to the stage. Accompanying deities had the heads of a deer or a cow and played various ceremonial instruments, hemming in the demons in the middle. They captured them and drove them away to waves of satisfaction and glee. The entire proceedings were like one great dance drama. The costumes were gaudy and multicoloured; peculiar in design and replete with mysterious touches.

Sunny took up a pen and made an earnest note on the wall, *30th January – Lama Temple – Shooing away ghosts.*

Chapter Six:
Morning Glory, the Ramshackle Temple, and the Four Deities

The next day, I couldn't sleep and so rose before daybreak. Why? Mosquito bites. The pests buzzed around my ears all night. They would swoop down just as I was dozing off, hell-bent on stopping me from slumbering. The fleas on the *kang* were lively as well. They crawled about my middle, creeping and nipping. A network of red welts appeared, chewing away into my very being. Not everything in the countryside was good – these big welts for one. I was afraid that I wouldn't recover even if I scratched away for a fortnight. Second Auntie and my mother were still sound asleep. Last night, they had been cheeping away like little birds, which was even more of a nuisance than the mozzies.

Getting up so early, I had no clue what to do. I came to the outer courtyard. The weather was somewhat cool and the grass licked with dew. The flowers in Second Auntie's courtyard were all commonplace varieties. There was white-picotéed morning glory, four o'clock flowers, sunflowers, and cockscombs. After a night's rest, all the plants were high-spirited. The four o'clock flowers already bore black seeds. If you cracked open the husks they expelled pale dust that if it blew in your direction could leave a coating on your face for ages. Sun Shun'er's wife told me this secret. She should have passed it on to her own daughter – the bonny little lass who left us too soon. Who could have thought that this tiny girl was a bailiff from a past life? My heart grew heavy when she crossed my mind.

I cannot pinpoint the exact moment the sky in the west turned red. The clouds above were dyed with what looked like rouge. The houses, goliath trees, vegetable plots and ponds radiated red below the cloud cover. It appeared as if they had been limned in paint. The sky behind the trees was the most radiant. After a while, the sun began to climb above their branches. I fixed my eyes on the place in case I might miss its grand entrance. Soon a red spot emerged behind the trees. That was what the adults called the cap of the sun. It seemed loath to be separated from the earth. My eyes became blurred, filled with that gigantic egg yolk shuddering vertically in front of me. It felt neither close to the trees nor distant from them.

Sunny came running out from the courtyard with the yellow dog and asked me what I was up to. I said I was watching the sunrise.

With just one turn of my head, the sun relinquished the tree boughs and pitched into the sky. The ground became golden bright. Even the leaves shuddered with a metallic sound when the wind blew. In that brightness, facing the sun, showering in the morning breeze, I found that I had grown clearheaded and all was transparent. It was as if I could now levitate. Bowing my head, I found that the yellow dog's expression had also become sacred. Its dark eyes scintillated beneath the sunlight.

At this critical juncture, I had an urge to compose an ode after the habit of my father. Only in this way might I give the sun its due. My father loved to write verse. He put pen to paper when he saw the moon, came across chrysanthemums, spied somebody selling tiny goldfish, or spotted a kite being flown. He wrote a poem to accompany almost every one of his paintings. Now, witnessing the rising of the sun, how could I not write a poem to be its companion? It should not be allowed to ascend in a solitary state. I told Sunny that I was going to create a verse for the sun at Sun Palace. "You are like the Emperor!" Sunny exclaimed.

I asked how that could be so? Sunny told me that Second Xia of the Xia family said: "One day the Emperor Qianlong was carrying out an inspection in the east and came over here. He happened to catch the dawn. He then looked down at the ground and saw an amazing glow reflected on it. The Emperor was as moved as I am now." He composed a poem likening this spot to the Palace of the Sun. Later, the villagers constructed a temple here and named it the Sun Palace.

"How come this Second Xia knows everything?"

Sunny related how Second Xia had studied in an old-style private academy. His was a family of intellectuals. I poured scorn on that, saying that Xia himself probably couldn't even get through the *Three Character Primer*.

"Maybe not."

I pleaded with Sunny to take me to see the Sun Palace. Sunny said that it was right behind me. I turned around, but could not find the red walls and golden tiles of a palace. Rather, there was an abandoned, dilapidated courtyard. At the doorway to the concourse stood a screening wall of indeterminate pattern, the adobe brick interior exposed to the outside. A twisted tree in low spirits was painted on the remaining surface. I wasn't sure if this was the Chinese hibiscus my father identified as the resting place of the sun. Two ancient elm trees grew in front of the courtyard and behind the house was an ailing willow. Together with the three tilted-roofed, single-storey rooms and a broken bell half-buried in the earth, everything seemed withered and deformed.

I said: "The Emperor's temple ought to have glazed tiles like the Lama's does. The top of the house should be painted gold so that it lives up to its name." Sunny claimed not to know what a glazed tile was and was certain that he'd never seen one.

The Sun Palace was not the Emperor's temple; rather, it was built by the villagers for their own use. Every year on 1st February the sun celebrated its birthday. Some of the faithful would come and light incense. That was all. "The sun is even more pitiful than the weasel," I judged. "It has such a grand name but is forced to live in such a small den. It really is unfair."

"This is much better than the shrine for the Village God. That one doesn't even reach up to my knee."

Entering the door of this "palace", the interior was more barren that the outside. The grass was half the height of a man and the ground heaped with broken clods, refuse, and dung. A decaying snake was draped along the steps, surrounded by a lively battalion of ants. The roofs of the three small lofts gaped open to the sky. On the northern wall was a two-foot high earthen platform upon which sat the statues of four deities with misshapen arms and legs. Their clay dermis was flayed off and their faces, which had been crudely and roughly modelled in the first place, had caved in. Unsightly in anybody's eyes.

I prayed tell who these four idols represented. Sunny knew via Second Xia that they were the Gods of the Sun, the Moon, Water and Fire.

Second Xia again!

"The Sun Palace should be set aside for the sun. Why did those other three join the party?"

Sunny suggested that they had perhaps come along as company, so the sun would not be lonely.

I couldn't deduce which of the quartet was the God of the Sun. The God of the Sun should be the sole master of this "grand temple". Sunny added that he didn't know either; nor did any of the villagers.

I felt quite disappointed by the Palace of the Sun. It laid waste to my hopes and expectations of what a palace should be. The ramshackle Sun Palace made me determined to show Sunny the Lama Temple. I must let him see how grand and magnificent and how specious a genuine palace is. Although silly Sunny knew how to bag fish and weave baskets, his horizons were narrow.

After breakfast, my mother and I were about to set off back home to the city. Sunny carried over the basket he had woven the night before. It was a delicate wicker ingot. Inside, there was a golden pumpkin, purplish black aubergines and violet-rooted pheasant's necks, along with four spotty-skinned sweet melons. In addition to the vegetables was half a bag of cracked corn and twenty free range eggs. We found it an effort to carry all this bounty.

Second Auntie and Sunny escorted us to the Eastern Dam River. En route, Sunny grilled me relentlessly about my ode to the sun. I promised that next time I would bring it over for him to read. He complained that he couldn't wait until then. He would come with his father to Theatre Stage Lane and the Lama Temple.

Father and son left us after they saw us climb onto the rickshaw. The yellow dog tailed our vehicle for some distance.

Chapter Seven:
Brine Stew, Driving Away the Ghosts, and Scarlet Fever

At the end of January, Second Uncle and Sunny came over with the expressed intention of watching the ghosts being driven away in the Lama Temple.

The father and son of the Cao family had made judicious preparations. Their clothes were all brand new. Second Uncle wore a long black robe, his belt fashioned from tawny cloth. Sunny's underclothes were short, yet his cotton-padded jacket and trousers were newly-made as well. Both balanced an identical trilby on their head and in a single glance you could tell they were purchased at the same time in the same place. Sunny's outer garments were obviously over-sized as the trouser bottoms and sleeves were rolled up. This was Second Auntie's idea. They might be on the large side now, but would come to fit as he grew into them.

Old Zhang led them to the reception room of the grand hall. They put down all the things they had brought from Sun Palace on the decorated tile floor. These included joints of mutton, an old hen whose wings were still flapping, some cabbages, a basket of eggs, and, of course, a bundle of tender green leeks wrapped in Second Auntie's cotton vest. Second Uncle was now more reserved and withdrawn than he had been in Sun Palace. Standing there rubbing his palms together, he didn't know how to conduct himself properly. My mother beckoned him to take a seat. He stared at the carved wooden armchair, hesitating for a long time before gingerly planting half of his posterior on it. It seemed as if he was ready to spring to his feet at any second. Sunny stood behind his father's chair with his arms folded and hands tucked into his sleeves. He was dumbfounded by the four painted scrolls on the wall. They were the handiwork of Old Seven, executed in the "elaborate style". The piebald cat beneath the peonies was modelled on our domestic moggy, and proved remarkably true-to-life. No matter at which angle you stood, its feline eyes always followed you. Peerless! Sunny, with his mouth wide open and his eyes staring, appeared too foolish to be a fool.

I ferried some tea over for the father and son from Sun Palace. It was fragrant jasmine from the Wu Yufen Teashop in Beijing. Second Uncle was shocked at how tiny the cup was. He mulled over it for a long time and, in the end, those hands more accustomed to harvesting leeks didn't take hold of the dainty winding handle.

The pair said they had already eaten their meal. My mother asked them to what meal they were referring and they replied lunch. She knew that they had gone without supper, so arranged a repast in the southern wing adjacent to the entrance hall. Usually it was uninhabited, though occasionally when my father's students dropped by and stayed too late to go out of the city, they would bed down there overnight. It did not contain a stove and, as with everywhere in Beijing at the time, did not possess central heating. Most households relied on stoves cast from imported iron. Families of refined taste would install smoke flues, lighting the fire in the courtyard and then, once the flame had banked up sufficiently, moving the stove indoors. Rooms at that time always seemed to be choking with the dense smell of coal.

That day, my mother didn't light up a stove for Second Uncle. Owing to the war, coal mined in the Western Hills could not be hauled into the city, leaving every home with only a limited supply. On those Beijing days when water droplets still formed into ice, how hard it must have been for the father and son who were used to sleeping on the warm *kang* in Sun Palace. Old Zhang remarked: "A stupid chap sleeps on a cold *kang* simply because he is strong in essence." His words made me feel rather disconsolate.

Our cook Old Wang steamed some corn cake and boiled a wok of cabbage for the pair. Although the food was plain and simple, it nevertheless proved hot and heartening. Second Uncle and Sunny were extremely content with the fare and made do with eating off the chopping board in the kitchen. Their heads were perspiring all over. Old Zhang mouthed off again: "Eat whenever you sweat, pocket only regret."

"You chatterbox, Old Zhang," I scolded. "How can you have so many words to say? They are my mother's guests and they are my guests too."

Old Zhang hailed from the countryside and once farmed in the Zhang Family Village. By now, he had been in the city for dozens of years. How could he have come so far that he now looked down his nose at fellow countryfolk? I despised him for his snobbery.

Second Uncle heaved a sigh of relief when he heard that my father had taken his students sketching at Jiming Station in Hebei Province. Sunny stated that if he had known about this he would have brought his mother to have a stroll about the Lama Temple too. Second Uncle countered: "If your mother had come with us, who would take care of the chickens and the dog?"

"It wouldn't harm them to skip a couple of meals."

They would parry away in this way, but when he saw my seventh brother – a senior sibling from my father's first marriage – he fell into dutiful silence. The business of Sunny's ma coming was no longer mentioned as he might very well treat this country woman with derision.

The duo ran into Old Seven, who had just returned home, in the courtyard. When Sunny learned that the fellow standing before him was the creator of the peonies and the cat, he instantly showered him with limitless respect and adoration. When Old Seven learned that the fellows standing before him farmed vegetables at Sun Palace, he simply nodded his head without even offering a verbal greeting. On seeing how he stalked to the rear of the courtyard without turning his head, I shouted: "Hey, Old Seven. Freeze!"

Old Seven asked me what the matter was.

Still, he didn't turn his head. Too proud of himself.

"Sun Cao wants you to teach him how to paint. He's been waiting more than half a year for this chance."

Slowly, Old Seven turned around. Not looking at Sunny's face, which was full of expectation, he piped up in a measured yet haughty way: "Want to learn to paint? Go to the Fine Arts Institute. That's where people learn to draw. I don't take on pupils. I'm not a house painter who can churn out golden dragons for wooden panels."

Let Sunny sit the entrance examination at Xu Beihong's Art Institute! How could he say that?

Sunny was saddened by Old Seven's reluctance and scorn. He bowed his head silently and rubbed the ground with his toe. I thought that he must feel dejected and sad in his heart. Usually Old Seven didn't set much store by who was junior and who was senior. He didn't discourage me from bullying and admonishing him. I hadn't expected that he would put on such airs and give our guests from the countryside the cold shoulder. Now he really had made me lose face.

The most disappointed soul of all must have been Sunny. He had arrived in high spirits, anxious to learn painting techniques from Old Seven. However, his warm cheeks were met with a cold backside. How could I brag about Old Seven's painting to Sunny anymore? Unexpectedly, Sunny raised his head, looked at me, smiled and noted: "Today, Brother Old Seven must be too tired."

I told my mother: "Your highness. You should say something to Old Seven. How could he act like that?"

My mother was only able to smile like Sunny. She was Old Seven's stepmother. A stepmother is known as a "later mother". How, indeed, could a later mother say anything to an earlier mother's son? She couldn't say one syllable.

You see, in our home only my mother and I took the Cao family as our kin. All the other relatives acted differently. No wonder Second Uncle was usually unwilling to visit us.

I believe that people should measure their own heart against those of others. In the summer when I went to Sun Palace, the entire Cao family received us with sincerity and honesty. I could find no fault in them at all. Now, they had come to our home and we treated them to boiled cabbage, made sarcastic comments and mocked them. I felt ashamed for my mother. How dare we darken the doors of Sun Palace again? It appeared that my mother didn't care about this. She had her own methods. I saw her secretly slip Sunny ten silver dollars and tell him he could buy whatever food caught his fancy outside. Ten silver dollars! That truly was a fortune. I doubt that my Second Auntie and Uncle could make this sum through a year's hard labour. Thus, both Second Uncle and Sunny were overjoyed. They didn't gripe about their reception. Despite being treated coldly and mocked sarcastically, they had money in their pockets.

Father and son spent the whole of the next day sightseeing. They recounted how they had been to the Bridge of Heaven, had watched people turning acrobatic tricks, and seen a brown bear juggling a pitchfork. They had also bought some velvet flowers and patterned material for Second Auntie's birthday. The cloth had green blossoms on an indigo ground. It was tacky and vulgar. I wondered how, when Sunny had aspirations in the fine arts field, he could have bought such a thing for his mother.

Second Uncle observed that Sunny had wolfed down six rounds of baked wheaten cake with soup. The peddler was so taken aback that he refused to sell him a seventh. Baked wheaten cake is a local delicacy in Beijing. Strictly speaking, it originates from Hebei Province. The method of preparation involves boiling the cake and pork together in a wok of brine. When you eat it, you lift the cake out of the pan and quarter it before ladling the soup into bowls. The pork melts in the mouth and the cake tastes moreish. Among ordinary people, this was a popular and tasty dish. It is a pity that, even to this day, I have never savoured this delicacy in Beijing. Every time I pass the small stands in the city I am enticed by the scent, but the sight of the colossal greasy wok and the mysterious objects boiling away in it deadens my appetite. It is hard to imagine how Sunny could have polished off six bowlfuls of cake and soup. How big his stomach must have been.

Compared with the twenty wheat-ear fish I consumed,

Sunny really did overindulge. At first, he thought nothing was amiss. Later, his belly expanded and expanded. Old Wang advised him to poke his tongue until he vomited, but Sunny couldn't bear to do that. Instead, he tried to weather the discomfort. At last, my mother employed the remedy she used for dealing with me. She asked Old Wang to dissolve bicarbonate of soda in half a bowl of water and make Sunny tip it down the hatch. Then Sunny managed to sleep, albeit with some effort.

The third day was the time for the driving away of ghosts at the Lama Temple. My mother wouldn't let me go and watch. She claimed that the whips the lamas swung to exorcise spirits flew about in a crazy fashion. Every year, some people ended up with lash injuries. When my father was away nobody could control me. My mother refused to let me attend and she would not attend either. She requested that Old Zhang accompany the father and son to the Lama Temple, ordering explicitly that they should just take a peek and not stay until the end. The weather was bitterly cold. They should be wary of frostbite. That whole morning I regretted not being able to go with Sunny to see the ghosts being driven away. I sincerely hoped that the lamas would be seized up with cold, rendering them unable to perform the ceremony.

When Old Zhang and the father and son left, floating snowflakes seasoned the sky. Northerly winds began to pierce people's napes. The temperature suddenly plummeted. Within an hour, the houses, trees and courtyard all became white. Nobody walked through the courtyard and it was tranquil. The piebald cat trotted across the snow, leaving behind a series of dainty plum-like prints. My mother lit a portable stove and let me warm my hands on it. She declared proudly: "Wasn't it better that you didn't go? At home, it's warm and snug. What's so interesting about watching ghosts being driven away in the Lama Temple in a blizzard? If you weren't careful you might have brought the ghouls back home with you."

The sound of the gong and the drums and the dismal whimper of the huge bronze bugle were couriered over from the west by the winds and snow. The call of the bugle was low yet resonant and stirred people's hearts. It seemed that the whirling snow was floating and dancing down from the sky with the assistance of the bugle. My mother's way of thinking was too simple and narrow. How could she understand the seductive appeal of what was unfolding in the Lama Temple to a little girl? The dancing over there was frenetic with striking colours, grotesque designs and exaggerated gestures.

Just after the alarm clock had completed two revolutions, Old Zhang brought Cao senior and junior back. He said that if he didn't return, Sunny would be sure to perish. My mother hurriedly asked what the matter was. Second Uncle recounted that Sunny's soul had been captured by the white ghost.

When we looked at Sunny behind Old Zhang, his head and body were dredged with white powder. His teeth were clamped tight shut and his eyes blank. His whole body shuddered. He did not answer my mother's questions. Instead, he only gritted his gnashers. My mother concluded that he must be possessed by a ghost. The lama had driven the ghost into his body.

Old Zhang said that Sunny had squeezed his way enthusiastically to the front and positioned himself very close to the stage. How could he have dodged the fatal powder?

My mother rushed over to pat the pale substance from his body. Old Zhang implored her to stop. He maintained that the white stuff would spread bad luck anywhere it landed. She then asked what we ought to do. Old Zhang thought he should be taken outside and dusted off in the street so any ill fortune would be trodden on by passersby and carried away with them.

"That's what they call 'using your neighbour's field as a drain'," I said. "Rather wicked."

"When we've run into this problem ourselves, it's not a case of being wicked or not," Old Zhang added. "Who could have imagined this would have befallen us?"

Like a puppet being manipulated in public by a travelling entertainer, Sunny found himself being hauled outside onto the street by Old Zhang and Second Uncle. He was patted for some time on the snow-covered ground until he blinked as if he had nodded off and become witless. Second Uncle implored: "Sunny, Sunny, say a word or two."

From beginning to end, Sunny didn't utter a single sound.

My heart went out to Sunny as I hadn't expected matters to take such a turn when he went to watch the ceremony. "Sunny comes from a poor down-at-heel family," Old Zhang reflected. "His fate is too lean and no higher than the dirt. This kind of auspicious spectacle is too much for him to handle. Those evil spirits who were driven and pranced about the square were bound to make a beeline for him."

My mother told Old Zhang not to blather anymore about it. The more he went on, the queerer the situation would become. She instructed Old Wang to boil a wok of piping hot ginger soup and forced the father and son to drink it. At midnight, Sunny was seized with a fever. Blisters broke out around his lips and he began to burble deliriously nonstop. My mother reasoned that last night he had eaten too much wheaten cake and brine soup. Suddenly stopping eating must have brought on his cold. Thus, she went to the pharmacy at the entrance to the lane and purchased a big heap of charred wheat shoots, hawthorn and medicated leaven. This she boiled and fed to Sunny.

The herbal infusion had no effect whatsoever. In the afternoon, Sunny's body was completely red and coated with pimples.

Old Zhang contended that this was called the "demon's pimples" and it was certain that Sunny was a victim of possession.

My mother beseeched Old Zhang to find a way of driving the evil spirit away. Old Zhang and Second Uncle braved the blizzard to venture to the Burning Temple in the east.

Old Zhang sought out Guangyu as he thought that he alone could work out how to save the child's life. On hearing the story, Guangyu refused and professed that he could do nothing. He directed them to find a better qualified master. After Old Zhang came back and reported this rebuttal, Old Wang rasped: "He was bound to give you the brush off. The lamas brought on this trouble, but you asked a monk to solve it. No wonder he recommended you consult a better qualified master."

In a moment of desperation, I invited Old Seven to come over. Old Seven was a learned man, better-informed than my mother. After all, my mother was illiterate. Old Seven stood for a long time before Sunny's bed and concluded: "This is no common-or-garden ailment. It shouldn't be tackled in just any old way." After speaking these words, he donned his overcoat and went through the snow to the south of the city to engage a doctor. Standing in the doorway, looking at Old Seven's shadow fading into the tumult, I sensed that I had maltreated him earlier. Actually, Old Seven had great solicitude towards Sunny and was not as glacial as I formerly judged him.

The doctor Old Seven summoned was Peng Yutang, an aged family friend who had once attended to me. Having trained in surgery overseas, he was adept at cerebral medicine. One time, somebody requested that he perform their operation. The fee was calculated in gold ingots. Of course, our family had none of these. He was willing to come over simply for my father's sake. They had been classmates.

Peng Yutang examined Sunny and diagnosed that he was suffering from an acute infectious disease – scarlet fever.

Scarlet fever is a condition which normally affects youngsters. My mother was scared when she heard the diagnosis. She was even more petrified than when she thought that ghosts had entered our door. Before the New Year, a kid in our lane by the name of Xiaoming died from this illness. After Xiaoming's death, some people wearing white surgical gowns sprayed medicated water over all the children in every family. Old Seven commented that this was acting blindly. There was no use in spraying them because scarlet fever was transmitted through saliva. My mother maintained that spraying them must be better than nothing. She specifically asked that they disinfect the front and rear of our courtyard. Whatever they might say, scarlet fever was a source of panic back then.

As soon as my mother hired a rickshaw and sent the two Caos back to Sun Palace, she put me into isolation in a small room and refused to let me go outside. She alleged that the virus Sunny had been infected with was still floating actively about the chamber. If I went down with it I was certain to die like Xiaoming. Every day, my mother examined my throat and took my temperature. Even the howl of the wind and the shriek of the birds unnerved her. If I let out so much as a light *paff*, she would urge Old Seven to fetch Peng Yutang. Isolated as I was in that small room, I tried every means imaginable to agitate my mother. Today, I might say I had a headache and tomorrow I might say that my body itched. The day after that I could complain of being bloated. I loved to see her panicked reaction. I loved to perceive that she had her heart in her mouth and that there was no one part of me she could scratch to alleviate my suffering.

All at once I had become the centre of my family's attention, as if I was grievously sick and would not survive for very much longer. I also convinced myself that my time could be measured in days, so passed on my wishes to my mother in whatever ways I could. Today I would say I wanted to eat steamed egg custard, tomorrow I would crave walnut brittle, and the day after that I would require steamed cake and boiled fish.

Old Seven told my mother: "Release her. You have been spoiling her too much. She's lost all sense of decorum."

Chapter Eight:
Paper Socks, Paper Shoes, and Second Uncle

More than half a year passed by in a flash. It was once again the end of summer and autumn was setting in. The waste paper I saved for Sunny had formed a stockpile. When I went with Old Seven to the secondhand bookshop he even bought a guide to painting for the lad. The book included prototypes of radishes, cabbages, crickets and morning glory and so forth. I thought that I would soon head for Sun Palace with my mother.

Unexpectedly, before we were to set out, Sunny came over by himself. He didn't take a rickshaw, but walked all the way. His body was a mass of greasy sweat and dust. Most shockingly of all, he was dressed in freshly-made mourning clothes. In the midst of the summer heatwave, the fabric on the crown of his head signified the loss of one of the most beloved members of the Cao family. That must be why he had these hemp mourning garments on. Once he entered, Sunny began to kowtow. He kowtowed to Old Zhang, to Old Wang, and even to me. My mother dashed outside and screamed: "Oh Sunny, what's happened?"

"My dad is gone."

"Wasn't he in rude health in January?"

"Last night he breathed his last."

On hearing that, my mother grabbed Sunny and ran towards the door. While running, she shouted for Old

Zhang to hire a rickshaw immediately. Old Seven handed some money to her, telling her that this was necessary. My mother accepted it, but looked stupefied. She took Sunny to the rickshaw and promised the rider whatever fee he desired as long as he sprinted as fast as his legs could carry him. I chased the vehicle out of the gate like the yellow dog, shouting: "Ma, ma, I should be with you too!"

My mother turned around and snapped: "Stay at home and behave yourself."

How was I to catch up with the rickshaw? I could see my mother's and Sunny's backs as they approached the entrance to the lane, then they turned to the south and disappeared.

The funeral at Sun Palace was a simple affair. My mother was back the following day. The master of the Cao family had died, Second Auntie had now been left a widow, and Sunny was a child without a father. It turned out that the scarlet fever that struck Sunny in January didn't spread to me, but infected his father instead. This suggests that if an adult goes down with it, the consequences are more grievous than for a child. Not long after he became ill, the condition reached Second Uncle's kidneys. His body was swollen and his urine bloody. They say that the disease is at its gravest when the patient experiences chronic fatigue. But how could Second Uncle – a vegetable farmer – permit himself to take a rest? The livelihood of the family depended entirely upon him.

Despite his renal failure, Second Uncle struggled off the *kang* and into the field. The crops failed to thrive and his health gradually deteriorated until he reached rock bottom.

It was reported that when he was put in his coffin his head was engorged to the size of a kneading tub. People could not make out his eyes and nose. His feet were so swollen that socks and shoes could not be wrenched onto them. Hence, his corpse had to wear stockings and footwear fashioned from paper.

Decades later, I qualified as a doctor, specialising in infectious diseases. What happened to Second Uncle Cao in no way directly influenced my decision. I worked in an infectious disease clinic in the North-West for eight years, where I treated countless patients for scarlet fever, adults and children alike. Some of them even developed glomerular nephritis, yet all made a full recovery. Today, with the advancement of medical science, this disease is no longer a threat to human life. When faced with this kind of patient, however, I would always bring to mind the picturesque countryside of Sun Palace, the paper stockings and shoes Sunny's father wore in his coffin, and his tobacco pipe and basket.

Within a year of Sunny's father's death, Second Auntie celebrated fresh nuptials. She had managed to find a step-father for Sunny. My mother, as her maternal kinswoman, was sure to attend the wedding. On the way there, my mother drilled it into me that when I arrived at Sun Palace I should wear a merry expression and only sweet words should issue forth from my mouth. Lucky phrases should be spouted in abundance. Late Uncle Cao ought not to be mentioned. The most critical thing was that I should address the newcomer as "Second Uncle". The greeting ought to trip off the tongue and not sound at all stilted. In this way, my new Second Uncle would be happy and my Second Aunt would feel relieved. Only if we pulled this off, could we be said to have not come in vain.

My mother asked me if I understood. I replied "no".

"You are already a primary school pupil. How can you not understand the ways of the world? Your Second Auntie is a woman with a kid. How could she survive in the countryside alone? If she didn't move on that would spell the end of the family. You should put yourself in her shoes."

My mother teared up while she was talking.

"Who is Sunny's new daddy?"

My mother said it was Second Xia from Xia Family Garden.

I raised my eyebrows and let out a cynical breath through puckered lips.

"Look at your attitude. What I hate most of all is when you make that peeping sound. How did Second Xia offend you?"

I didn't let out a single word all the way there.

Speechless.

Everything was the same: the earthen house, the fences, the chicken coop, and the gourd trellis. Referring to them as the Caos was utterly prohibited. Now I had to address the Xia family.

The Xia family wedding was uncomplicated, even slipshod. They just prepared a large wok of brine noodles. Guests could be served straightaway. The soup was exceedingly salty. Half a ladle would make people gag on their noodles. Second Auntie was decked out in her floral purple coat – the cloth bought by her late husband in January. Nobody could have conceived that it would be put to use on this particular occasion. Second Xia had on a long blue robe – he wore it to convey that he had once studied for half a session in an old-style private academy. In other words, he was the spawn of a family of intellectuals. My mother gave her greetings and blessings to Second Aunt, yet when her back was turned she secretly dabbed away her tears. Second Auntie's eyes were red as well. She affected a smile as she crammed brown sugar cake into my hands.

Second Xia's physique was sturdy, with a bald pate, a

goatee beard and moustache, and slightly-tilted eyes. You could never discern who exactly he was looking at. It was mind-boggling. Second Xia received us with an exaggerated greeting. He declared that we were his kinsmen from the extended family in the big city. He boasted that once when he sent vegetables to the artillery factory in the Northern Street he had passed our household. The mighty gate, those huge beams, the exalted steps, and the horse-mounting stones all denoted that we were a high-ranking family. It was wonderful now, he announced, that whenever he tramped to the artillery bureau he would have a place where he could rest his feet and sip tea. While talking, he offered me a pear. The fruit was overly big, so he sliced out a section for me. I accepted it, but discreetly plopped it on the windowsill. Such a happy day, yet eating a pear then would not have been an auspicious omen.

I disliked this man named Second Xia. He was too verbose and his slanting eyes too energetic. Set alongside the former Second Uncle, I found that Cao was still my favourite. From the outset until the end, I refrained from calling Second Xia my Second Uncle. My mother belted me repeatedly, though I could not force my mouth into doing her bidding. Impossible.

That day I discovered Sunny in the small temple named the Sun Palace. He was sitting at the feet of the four deities, huddling his hands around his knees. His eyes were dopey and his face blanched. Gone was the glow and vitality of days past. On seeing me, his first words were: "I killed my father."

"How can you think like this? You shouldn't."

"It was me who passed the disease on to him. If he hadn't gone down with it, he wouldn't have died. He was a strapping fella. Whatever happens to me, I deserve to be punished."

"That's not the full story. Old Zhang always says that life and death are a matter of destiny; wealth and honour depend on the heavens. The heavens arrange things like that. Who is able to ignore the will of the heavens?"

Sunny buried his head in his arms. I envisaged his tearful, agonised face. On his mother's happy day and the arrival of his new father, tracks streamed down Sunny's face. I told him to attend kindly to his mother as she was a pitiful woman.

"What does she have to be pitiful about? She has a new man again and is happy."

After a while, Sunny resumed: "Do you know, now I'm no longer named Sun Cao. My name is Sun Xia."

"I will still address you as Sun Cao and call you Sunny."

Sunny waved his head and scoffed: "Hey, this is a humble name. Whatever I am called makes no difference."

"We are not humble at all. The sun shines with boundless radiance. How can that be called humble?"

"I have no father and no mother either. A child without a father and mother is lower than a blade of grass."

"What are you talking about? Your mother is your true mother."

"The grass over my daddy's grave hasn't grown this high … and she has married again."

I mimicked my mother's tone and proclaimed: "She is a woman. How could she survive alone? If she didn't remarry that would spell the end of the family."

"Haven't you noticed? The family has already fallen apart."

"Sunny, I won't be able to visit you so often. I've started to go to school. Later on, if you can grab the chance, come to Theatre Stage Lane and look for me. Old Seven has promised that he will teach you to paint. He's bought you a book too."

Sunny smiled bitterly and said nothing.

I kept Sunny company in the Sun Palace for half a day. My mother came over for me and said we were going back to the city. Both Second Auntie and my mother knew that we could no longer come and stay. The master of the family had changed.

Sunny sat in the ramshackle temple, the four deities as his companions. He didn't return until we were about to leave. "Sunny is too stubborn," Second Auntie reflected. "He has too many things weighing on his mind."

My mother tried to reassure her by observing: "As time goes on, it will gradually get better."

"Kids in the countryside still have hearts and lungs all the same," I chipped in.

My mother told me not to fling oil on the flames. Second Auntie's heart was already too fragile.

Chapter Nine:
Resist US Aggression, Aid Korea, Volunteer for the Army

From that time onwards, largely because I was unable to follow my own volition, I had no chance to visit Sun Palace again. I started to attend school in the Fang Family Lane and was no longer the wild, unbridled foal I had once been. The bit had been slid between my teeth. During this period though, my mother continued to travel to Sun Palace. Of course, that was for Second Auntie's sake.

Second Auntie died. She went very suddenly. It was reported that she slipped carelessly into the Kiln Pit and drowned.

"She had been living quite comfortably," my mother said in disbelief. "What business did she have going over there?"

Second Xia maintained that she had gone there searching for Sunny. Most of the time, she would trawl the village, bellowing out his name and looking high and low. Sunny could not brush along with other children, his disposition being silent and offbeat. People did not like to be in his company.

My mother wondered why her friend had gone to the Kiln Pit. To Second Xia's mind it was an unfathomable place, the denizen of drowned ghosts. They could not be reincarnated into a new body unless each year they dragged somebody new into the depths.

Even my mother dismissed that as "superstitious and beyond belief".

I believed that my Second Auntie could find no meaning in life and so chose to snuff it out. I heard from my mother that when her body was hauled from the pit she was wearing that same purple floral coat she had worn on her wedding day. The red velvet flower was still pinned to her head. She had braided it tightly into her hair, lest it become detached. It appeared that everything had been organised.

According to Old Zhang's analysis, when Sunny was doused in white powder at the Lama Temple it initiated his fixation with ghosts. His personality became muddled and, as a result, he was struck by one misfortune after another. This had been ordained by the God of Death in the Underworld. I thought he was spouting nonsense.

Soon, Second Xia went on to marry again. He now had a son of his own and named him Morning Sun Xia.

Sunny was genuinely without a father or a mother.

In 1952, during the War of Resisting US Aggression and Aiding Korea, Sunny joined the volunteer army.

Upon his departure, he made a point of visiting our family to bid farewell. Sunny appeared mighty and handsome in his military uniform. He was no longer the dispirited youth huddled at the feet of the four deities. I touched his new outfit and big fur hat.

With admiration I told him: "The pupils in our schools are preparing little pouches containing words of encouragement for the soldiers fighting at the front. We have written letters, made bookmarks, donated towels and notebooks and suchlike to the school. They will then send them to Korea. Everybody hopes that their bag might find its way into the hands of a hero. How lucky and special that would be."

Sunny replied that he didn't want a towel. He wished that the bag he got would have a book on painting inside. I asked him how he could apply the same mind to both fighting and reading. He must protect our country and guard our homeland.

My mother interrupted me from one side: "Sunny, are you really going to leave Sun Palace?"

"Auntie, I really am leaving."

"After you've left, won't you miss your home?"

"Is there anything worth missing there?"

The next words my mother spoke astonished me. My mother instructed Sunny to be smart when fighting at the front because a bullet has no eyes. She told him not to shoot anybody in places where it could prove fatal. Every person's life is a life.

My mother was then an active member, and director, of the Public Security Committee. Her words as a director to a volunteer soldier going to the front made me understand her in a new way. My mother exposed the other side of her personality to Sunny without any reservation. Maybe she possessed some powers of telepathy? When she showed her face to me, she was always the hard and firm director.

The day Sunny was due to leave our home, he suddenly recalled something which he passed onto me. "The small temple which housed the Sun Palace has been renovated. It's a primary school now."

"What about the four deities."

"They were thrown into the Kiln Pit and dissolved into mud."

Sunny left for Korea.

One year passed, and then two and three. I received no message from him.

One group of soldiers returned, and then two and three. I still found not a shadow of him.

By the end of 1958, all the volunteer soldiers had returned. Even so, I received no news of Sunny.

During the Cultural Revolution, I ran into Second Xia. He was now a white-haired, lousy dodderer with his back arched and shoes slouching off. He told me he was still living in the same old place. His younger son Morning Sun Xia was now an apprentice in the city and he had come to visit him. I asked him about the fate of Sunny. He claimed that there had been no communication; no communication at all.

After a pause, Second Xia went on: "Actually his surname is Cao and he has nothing to do with our Xia family."

Sunny had been tugged out at the roots.

"Sun Cao is bound to come back," I predicted.

Chapter Ten:
Missing Sunny

Through the decades, Beijing has altered greatly. It often happens that if you don't venture out onto the streets for several months, the place has changed beyond all recognition.

Owing to enforced relocation, our family found itself transplanted from Theatre Stage Lane to Wangjing District in the north-eastern quarter of the city. We now occupy the twenty-fifth floor of our building. Every day, we watch Beijing through the clouds and fog, gazing on as high structures spring up near and far. The more we watch, the more our view becomes obscured. Each day, I have to travel three stops on the city bus to buy vegetables at the morning market. The market is named the Xia Family Garden Market and alongside it stands the Sun Palace station of the Tenth Circle Line of the Metro. Amid the throng of the market, the Kiln Pit, the vegetable plots and Grandpa Xia's stone tablet have all been reconstituted into fresh fish and veggies and transfigured into glass greenhouses with busy peddlers. The peddlers have nothing to do with Second Xia, but the silhouette of each of them mirrors his likeness. A man with a goatee sells tomatoes. The price is double that of other vendors, his advertising slogan proclaiming that they were, "Produced from the traditional, local sand-flats". When he sees me drifting back and forth in front of his stall, the short-bearded chap says: "Buy a pound and take them back to try. You'll find they taste the same as when you were a nipper. I'm sure you'll come back tomorrow."

In the flower and bird market, somebody is selling hamsters. With great perseverance, the small creature endlessly spins around the wheel in its cage. This makes me recall what Sunny told me about the weasel practising its self-conditioning beneath the light of the moon. Five centuries is still a long time to go. Where does the weasel practise now? Has it so adjusted its regimen that it now kicks around a wheel?

The pink Chinese rose is now in full bloom in the flower urn – a sign of the metropolitan "greening" programme. Unconsciously, I spot a tender morning glory among the roses. The tiny blossom uncurls shyly and peeps at the outside world beyond the clump. By accident or design, I have run into the soul of Sun Palace. My heart is stirred again and again. There are sweet memories and bitter sadness. A pang of personal longing for the place seizes hold.

I wait at the bus stop with a bundle of greens in my hands. The tall, forest-like buildings around me rob me of my bearings. The sun rises from the east as a fuzzy red circle. No sooner has it exposed its cap than it disappears behind some skyscrapers. It seems shy about meeting its old friends. Sun Palace; the palace for the sun. Nowadays, who can remember its bygone image? I remember the ode that I wanted to compose for Sun Palace. Dozens of years have passed and I haven't yet finished writing it. The key problem is that, since then, I have never encountered such moving sunshine nor experienced that selfsame mood and primal excitement.

South Lake and South Lake Park are not far away. They may have been formed from quarries in much the same way as the old Kiln Pit. The scenery is still picturesque, the lawns being newly-laid and the mountains produced by landscaping. It lacks the wild profusion of the natural world. Waving its head and wagging its tail, a yellow dog bounds over from the opposite side of the street. I approach it with surprise and trepidation, but the hound pauses in front of me. Looking into its eyes, I find a glimmer of familiarity. I ask the master what type it is. "Labrador," he replies.

Oh, a foreign breed.

Raising my head, I stare up at the sun again. It has already hidden itself in the clouds, refusing to reveal its face. A knot of passengers unravel from the Sun Palace metro station. Could this station have been built on the exact site of the small temple of that name? Is that huge, glazed supermarket what has become of Sunny's former home?

Sun Cao, are you still in the world of the living?

9th September, 2013

A note on the text

Ye Guangqin has revisited her childhood in Beijing many times in her stories, but cautions readers that she is prone to exercising literary license in chronologies, geographical details and proper names.

The list of the nine sons of the dragon in Chapter One should be rounded out with Jiaotu (number six), Chiwen (number seven), and Pixu (number nine). Likenesses of Jiaotu are often to be found by large gates as he is the nightwatchman who wards off petty visitors, but can also assist those who aspire to learn or seek promotion or progeny. Chiwen is the guardian of the house who drives away domestic evil. Pixu is a fierce creature depicted as all mouth and no anus. The principle is that he accumulates wealth and fortune, letting not one iota pass through. Chinese shops frequently have a *pixu* sculpture near the door. This is a toad-like creature that has a coin balancing between its lips; its abdomen culminating in one tuberous limb. An alternative sequence names the offspring as Bixi, Chiwen, Pulao, Bi'an, Taotie, Baxia or Gongfu, Yazi, Suanni and Jiaotu or Shutu.

The Peng Yutang in *Sun Palace* appears to be the same doctor mentioned by Liu Zhengcai in *The Mystery of Longevity: Traditional Chinese Therapeutic Exercises and Techniques* (English translation published by Foreign Languages Press, Beijing, 1990). A silk-reeler by profession, he suffered a severe bout of tuberculosis at the age of forty-eight, recovered through learning *qigong* and then retrained as a practitioner of Traditional Chinese Medicine under a local pedagogue. In another story by Madame Ye, *The Spring of Yutang*, Master Peng is said to have retained the complexion of a thirty-year-old, despite being a centenarian.

Acknowledgements

The author and translators wish to thank Jamie McGarry and Valley Press for helping to bring this publication to fruition. Funding for the project was provided by Northwest University and China Classics International, while the publishing rights were granted by Taibai Arts and Literature Publishing House. Thanks are also due to Dr J. Graham Jones and Jo Heywood for their assistance with the proofreading.